The AB Club

Other books written by Michelle Whitaker Winfrey

Children's Books

It's My Birthday... Finally! A Leap Year Story, 2nd Edition

It's My Birthday... Finally! Activity & Workbook, 2nd Edition

It's Not Leap Year this Year! A Leap Year Story

Leap Year Apparel – www.cafepress.com/leap_year

Leap Year Apparel – www.cafepress.com/leaper

Religious Study

Yours, Mine and God's
Giving and Receiving:
All for the Love of God and the Church

Yours, Mine and God's Apparel – www.cafepress.com/YMG

Parenting

A Mom's Guide to Surviving High School Athletics

Proud Parent Apparel – www.cafepress.com/HSSports

More Apparel by Michelle

"You Deserve A Dull Moment"
www.cafepress.com/adullmoment

The AB Club
For the *Am•Bitious* Woman in You!

Michelle Whitaker Winfrey

The AB Club
For the *Am•Bitious* Woman in You!

Copyright © 2012 by Michelle Whitaker Winfrey
Cover Illustration © 2012 Joyce Mihran Turley
Cover Design and Layout by Joyce Mihran Turley, Dixon Cove Design

All rights reserved. No part of this book may be reproduced or utilized in any form or by any means electronic or mechanical, including photocopying, recording or by any information storage and retrieval system without permission in writing.

Hobby House Publishing Group
A Division of Blaque Design, LLC.
P.O. Box 1527
Jackson, NJ 08527

ISBN: 978-0-9727179 91

Library of Congress Control Number: 2012905573

Frog carrying mushroom with or without the double H is a Trademark of Hobby House Publishing Group, Inc.

Printed in the United States of America

For all the best friends…

Stay together
and support each other
through your **ambitions!**

Dedicated to

Trina Sumner ❖ Joanna Chapman ❖ Ruby Whittaker

Special Thanks

Karen Fayd'herbe de Maudave for the spark!

and

Jessica Bourgeois for her hours of proof reading.

Acknowledgements

I have been fortunate to have wonderful <u>ambitious</u> friends!

I thought it would be great to include their words of ambitious survival, so I asked them.

In their words, you will see how fortunate I am!

Trina (Back cover far left)
Joanna (Back cover right)
Ruby (Back cover left)

Lillian
Sarah
Jackie
Jennifer
Twelve

and Garry, Bob & Ed

Thanks for sharing your point of view

Website and more

www.michellewinfrey.com

Follow Michelle on Twitter @michellewinfrey

Like The AB Club on Facebook
"The AB Club"
For the Ambitious Woman in You

Blog with Michelle and share your Ambitiousness
www.michellewinfrey.blogspot.com

Contact Michelle at michelle@michellewinfrey.com

The AB Club
For the *Am•Bitious* Woman in You!

Contents

Introduction	15
How to Use This Book	19
Mission Statement	21

The AB Survival Skills

YOU	25
FAMILY	117
LOVE	151
FRIENDS	185
WORK	215
FAITH	255

Listing of Survival Skills

YOU: AB Survival Skills 1 – 121

FAMILY: AB Survival Skills 122 – 154

LOVE: AB Survival Skills 155 – 183

FRIENDS: AB Survival Skills 184 – 214

WORK: AB Survival Skills 215 – 255

FAITH: AB Survival Skills 256 – 287

The AB Club
For the *Am•Bitious* Woman in You!

Ambitious

Introduction

The Mission Statement for this book is written in a manner that may make one think that this book is a work of fiction, when in fact *The AB Club* is really a tool that women – and men – can adapt to help survive. I was really on my way to lunch with a friend when the concept for the book was developed. To be precise, we were on our way to our favorite Indian restaurant, and yes, we were complaining about the impossible things that happen at our jobs.

Part of my personal development was and still is my willingness to share my thoughts, knowledge, and occasionally my opinion with others. I learned that the more I shared, the more ambitious I became.

Over the past twenty years, this sharing blossomed into the opportunity to mentor several young people. My words to them appear throughout these pages.

I have developed three core values for mentoring that I will share with you, in hopes that you too with have the opportunity to mentor one day.

    1) Believe in yourself.

    2) Have a purpose or intent in life – beyond your job.

    3) Be secure in your religious beliefs.

You must know where your religious beliefs stand, because, they will come into play when mentoring. Not everyone I mentored has been a practicing Christian, and that is okay, because I am, and I have enough of God in me for the both of us. What I have learned by mentoring people of different faiths, is to have a greater respect for others beliefs, and to remain grounded in mine.

Most important, you do not need to be perfect to mentor. You must have the ability to be honest with yourself, so you can pass along your experiences and survival skills truthfully. You do not need to know everything to mentor. You must have the ability to admit what you do not know. You cannot be selfish and mentor, because mentoring requires that you give 100% of yourself to the person looking to you for guidance. And lastly, there is no schedule for mentoring… it is a responsibility that requires however much time the protégé requires. Some need very little, and some need a little bit more.

You cannot mentor if you are not ambitious!

I have been blessed to have had two fabulous, ambitious mentors. The first was my high school dance teacher, Maxine Meyers. What a blessing she was to a young girl inspiring to dance her way through life, without an understanding of life beyond the ability to dance. You see, to a talented 16-year-old, I was going to dance forever. She taught me that I had another gift inside me. I was blessed with the ability to lead and manage people and situations into positive outcomes. Now over thirty-five years later, I am still dancing; and also teaching, sharing and mentoring through dance. She taught me that the "dance" is my spirit. My dance spirit keeps me positive and keeps a smile on my face and laughter in my voice. The first survival skill in this book was taught to me by her: "Love, like and admire yourself."

My second mentor was Belinda Davis. I met her in between college and graduate school and actually worked as her secretary for a short while. She was a brilliant business woman, who mentored to me without thought or pause. Her words to me over the years have stayed with me to the point that I am repeating them to my protégés, and my son. The most important life survival skill I learned from Belinda is that "I am worthy." The second was that I do not need to change who I am for a man. If he wants me, he will accept me just as I am. This she taught me through a story of her own life experiences.

You will get the most out of your mentor if you are ambitious!

I love sharing what is in my heart and on my mind, with a preference to develop beyond me.

The AB Club pulls together all the important aspects of life: You, Family, Love, Work and Faith. You can take this book seriously and use it to help you find balance and happiness in your life or you can just have fun, and skim through it, finding the AB Survival Skills that make you laugh, cry, think or remind you of a situation that just makes you smile.

However you choose, just enjoy!

Michelle

How to Use This Book

**Monitor your personal
Am-Bitious Survival Skill level,
or as we call it, your Ambitiousness!**

How many AB Survival Skills have you mastered?

As you read through *The AB Club*, check off the "AB Survival Skills" you have utilized in your life. Then review and calculate your level of Ambitiousness.

Over time as you use and master new AB Survival Skills, go back and check them off too. Then recalculate your level of Ambitiousness.

Use the note pages at the end of each section to keep track of the AB Survival Skills you are working towards, and have set goals to achieve.

Note Pages

The note pages can also be used to record your feelings, thoughts and as a place to add your own survival skills. There is a questionnaire at the end of each section that is designed to get you to think about how you can further your ambitions and how you can share them.

There is no rush in taking this survey. You may choose to take them all when you finish the book or directly after you complete each section. However you choose is fine. Enjoy them and have a few "ah ha" moments!

Understanding your Ambitiousness Level

You will monitor your survival level per chapter. This will allow you to see which of the five areas you are strongest in and which need the most work. There are no failures here, only upward growth.

There is no level for 100% because we are "women," not perfect!

80% and more checked
Congratulations!
You are Am-Bitious Savvy. Keep up the good work and lots of luck and success in your life!

50% - 79% checked
Great Start!
You can clearly see what needs to be gained as an Am-Bitious woman, so make it happen.

Up to 49% checked
The future is yours!
Keep working towards being the best Am-Bitious woman you can.

Regardless of the level you are at, do not compare your scores with others. We are all at different places in our lives at different times.

This is your journey!

Mission Statement

The AMBITIOUS Club herein known as
The *AB Club*™
was founded on February 22
at approximately 12:30 in the afternoon
by two friends on their way to lunch.
Their conversation was fueled by gossip
- all true of course -
anger, humor, the need to survive
and an ambition to overachieve at
their present jobs, friendships,
marriages and life.

Ambitious they were!
Survive they will!
Dangerous they are!

Membership is available to all those
AMBITIOUS enough to turn the page.

…and here is their story
as they see it through a list of
Survival Skills
they developed & borrowed.

Several borrowed skills have been applied
so frequently that they can no longer tell them
apart from the ones they developed.

Our apologies if we borrowed yours
without giving you the credit.

You

Definition of YOU

You are an independent woman,
who is beautiful,
talented and ambitious!

AB Survival Skill #1

Love, like and admire yourself!

My mentor Maxine Meyers

AB Survival Skill #2

Take responsibility for your faults, errors and mistakes.

Then make room…
because there will be more!

AB Survival Skill #3

Bragging is not sexy!

AB Survival Skill #4

Do not let anyone borrow
or drive your car unless they
can afford to fix it.

Otherwise, be prepared
to pay the bill, or lose a friend.

Keep the friend
and your keys in your purse.

AB Survival Skill #5

Hug someone everyday!

AB Survival Skill #6

Be kind.

You will see the rewards.

AB Survival Skill #7

Your intuition is important!

Listen to it.

AB Survival Skill #8

Accept apologies quickly
and with grace.

AB Survival Skill #9

Enjoy compliments with a polite
"thank you" and a smile!

AB Survival Skill #10

Give out compliments
and make sure you really
mean them.

Insincerity has a strong smell.

AB Survival Skill #11

Get it off your chest
so you can move on.

So write it down, tear it up
and flush it.
Go outside and have a scream!

Now think about it and
approach the situation
without emotion.

Do not approach the situation
angry or upset.

AB Survival Skill #12

Negative people will hold you back.

Peel them off one at a time until you are completely surrounded by positive people only.

AB Survival Skill #13

Treat yourself to flowers.

AB Survival Skill #14

Make sure your weave is tight!

PS: You can define "tight."

AB Survival Skill #15

Allow yourself empathy
towards others.

AB Survival Skill #16

Detox.

It is not only good for your body,
but your mind and soul as well.

AB Survival Skill #17

Preventative medical and dental
care is worth every penny.

AB Survival Skill #18

If you lend someone your clothes or
shoes, remember they
will never fit the same again.

So, you might as well give them away.

AB Survival Skill #19

Smile!

A nice smile will open doors.

AB Survival Skill #20

Always keep a credit card with a zero or low balance for emergencies.

My friend Trina

AB Survival Skill #21

Keep emergency cash in the house.

NOTE: Those shoes you saw are not an emergency.

AB Survival Skill #22

It's okay to be cynical sometimes, but do your best to be open-minded and understanding.

My friend and protégé Sarah

AB Survival Skill #23

Treat yourself to at least one expensive handbag!

AB Survival Skill #24

When upset walk away.

Angry actions and words are never the best.

Ambitious

The desire to achieve.

AB Survival Skill #25

Have "thick skin!"
Not everything should be absorbed.

Some things, actually most things, need to just roll off.

AB Survival Skill #26

Always have birthday cake on your birthday. Celebrating your life is wonderful!

Don't worry about your age; everyone else is getting older too!

AB Survival Skill #27

Once you say it, it is out there.
You can apologize, but your words cannot be revoked.

So, don't say it!

AB Survival Skill #28

Being a woman is no excuse for a wimpy handshake.

AB Survival Skill #29

Keep "Let's Jam",
or your favorite hair gel,
in your overnight bag.

AB Survival Skill #30

Know what's going on in the world.
Watch the news, read a newspaper,
listen to it in your car,
or read it online.

AB Survival Skill #31

Excellence vs. perfection

Excellence is obtainable!

You will never be perfect.
So why live a life of failure?

AB Survival Skill #32

Understand money!
Not how to spend it,
but how it works.

AB Survival Skill #33

Pay cash as often as possible.

You will enjoy that new
couch more knowing that a
bill is not coming!

AB Survival Skill #34

Keep a clean house!

My friend Jackie

You never know who
might stop by!

AB Survival Skill #35

Forgive yourself for not being perfect!

AB Survival Skill #36

Life isn't tied with a bow, but it is still a gift.

My friend Joanna

AB Survival Skill #37

Always say "thank you."

AB Survival Skill #38

Forgive yourself for your imperfections,
because you will never
be perfect.

AB Survival Skill #39

Pay yourself every payday!

AB Survival Skill #40

Recycle!

AB Survival Skill #41

Living within your budget is more relaxing than pay bills.

It just takes a little work and commitment.

AB Survival Skill #42

Panty lines are not pretty.
Wear the right underwear.

AB Survival Skill #43

Have a bra fitting annually,
and every time you gain or lose
a lot of weight.

It's FREE!

AB Survival Skill #44

Always give it your best shot!

AB Survival Skill #45

Be culturally well rounded.

AB Survival Skill #46

Listen to different types of music.

The enjoyment of music crosses all cultures.

AB Survival Skill #47

Jealousy is real!

Recognize it in yourself and in others!

AB Survival Skill #48

Travel with duct tape.
You will be surprised how
useful it is!

Use it to fix…

The hem of your dress

The sole of your shoe

A rip in your coat

The strap of your handbag

Your suitcase…

and much, much more!

AB Survival Skill #49

Buy yourself something for Christmas. Wrap it and place it under the tree.

This way you are guarantee to get at least one thing that you want.

AB Survival Skill #50

If you have never had a mentor, find one. It's never too late.

AB Survival Skill #51

Be sure to laugh, everything is more entertaining that way!

My friend and protégé Sarah

AB Survival Skill #52□

Visit Washington, D.C.

AB Survival Skill #53□

Visit your state capital

AB Survival Skill #54

Register to vote.

AB Survival Skill #55

Vote.

AB Survival Skill #56

Make sure your passport is always up to date.

AB Survival Skill #57

Always have a personal
point of view.

So, what's yours?

AB Survival Skill #58

You can keep yourself down.
You can also pick yourself up.

AB Survival Skill #59

Find jeans that fit your body!

Not Your Daughters Jean:
one of my best discoveries!

AB Survival Skill #60

Learn to read between the lines!

My friend Jackie

AB Survival Skill #61

Sometimes the best and most important words are not spoken.

AB Survival Skill #62☐

Own red lipstick!

AB Survival Skill #63☐

Own a little black dress
and a string of pearls.

AB Survival Skill #64

Dress in the dark – just once –
then walk out of your house, with your
head held high, as though you are
starting a fashion trend.

It's liberating, because you
will understand that it is not the clothes,
but the woman in the
clothes that matters.

AB Survival Skill #65

Know how to check the oil in your car.

AB Survival Skill #66

You are a work in progress…
keep developing!

My niece Twelve

AB Survival Skill #67

Know what your talents are!

AB Survival Skill #68

What's on your "bucket list"?

Why Create a Bucket List?

Because it is a fun and serious way to set life goals.

AB Survival Skill #69

Always continue to learn for
self-knowledge and self-improvement.

My friend and protégé Lillian

AB Survival Skill #70

What more do you need than a "butter knife" in your tool box!

AB Survival Skill #71

Know how to describe yourself in three words or less.

AB Survival Skill #72

Sometimes your best is good enough, and sometimes your best needs to be better.

It is important to know the difference.

(Not sure where I heard this, but love it.)

AB Survival Skill #73

When asked to keep a secret, keep it.

AB Survival Skill #74

If you choose to tell your secrets, understand the character of the person you tell them to.

AB Survival Skill #75

Keep your secrets.
If you tell even one person, it is no longer a secret.

AB Survival Skill #76

Respect!

Yourself and Others!

My niece Twelve

AB Survival Skill #77

Embrace today!

AB Survival Skill #78☐

Save more in the bank
than you spend on your hair
and nails!

AB Survival Skill #79☐

Something is to be said for
taking a nap.

Why do we stop?

AB Survival Skill #80

Stand by your values and do not compromise them…
for anyone.

My friend and protégé Lillian

AB Survival Skill #81

Chocolate does make you
feel better.

AB Survival Skill #82

When you enter a room,
speak first!

When leaving a room,
say "good bye" first.

AB Survival Skill #83

Read and know what your favorite books are.

My favorite books are:

"All I Really Need to Know I Learned in Kindergarten"
by Robert L. Fulghum

"Way of the Peaceful Warrior"
by Dan Millman

"The Purple Cow"
Transform Your Business by Being Remarkable
by Seth Godin

AB Survival Skill #84

Always forgive,
but never forget!

AB Survival Skill #85

Don't try to have the body you had 20 years ago.
Try to have the best body you can have today.

AB Survival Skill #86

If you gain weight do not look for someone to blame.

Look for the reason why, and then work towards a change.

AB Survival Skill #87

Remember yesterday!
Look forward to tomorrow!

AB Survival Skill #88

Plan for tomorrow!

AB Survival Skill #89

Eat off the good dishes.
Don't save them for
company only.

AB Survival Skill #90

Travel whenever possible.

Start with the
United States of America.

AB Survival Skill #91

Broke like a joke,
but still spending!

If this is you… change NOW!

AB Survival Skill #92

Make peace with the past,
so it won't mess up
the present.

My friend Joanna

AB Survival Skill #93

Magazines are a great learning tool.
Know what your favorites are.

My favorite magazines are:

"Smithsonian Magazine"

and

"Money Magazine"

AB Survival Skill #94

Explore and enjoy the arts!

AB Survival Skill #95

In a competition someone always loses!

AB Survival Skill #96

Do not live in the past… always move forward.

AB Survival Skill #97

Choose your memories.
Bad memories will slow you
down and good memories
can fuel your future.

AB Survival Skill #98

If you eat when stressed,
nervous or upset eat as many raw
vegetables as you wish.

This way when you are finished,
you do not have the added
stress over what you just ate.

AB Survival Skill #99

If you love your size…
LOVE IT!

AB Survival Skill #100

Make time for exercise!

AB Survival Skill #101

Don't put it in writing, unless
you want it read.

This includes email, texting, blogging,
instant messaging,
and everything else that falls
in this bucket.

AB Survival Skill #102

Do not confuse being ambitions
with being that "other word"!

They are not the same.

AB Survival Skill #103

Learn to play Spades.

It can save a boring party!

AB Survival Skill #104

Mess up – fess up,
then move on!

AB Survival Skill #105

Go out to dinner alone.
It's a wonderful experience.

AB Survival Skill #106

Do not compare your life
to that of others.
You have no idea what their
journey is about.

My friend Joanna

AB Survival Skill #107

Learn a foreign language.

AB Survival Skill #108

Develop a budget and follow it.
Make sure it is realistic.

AB Survival Skill #109

Your attitude affects all aspects of your life!

AB Survival Skill #110

Learn to dance… any style!

AB Survival Skill #111

Learn to play an instrument… any type.

AB Survival Skill #112

Even when on a diet, always accept
birthday cake and take a bite.

It is a gracious act to
celebrate others.

AB Survival Skill #113

You can't always get what you want, but you can have loads of fun trying!

AB Survival Skill #114

Develop a protégé!

It's a very rewarding experience.

AB Survival Skill #115

Listen!

It is very important that we not only listen with our ears, but with our hearts and mind.

You may hear more.

AB Survival Skill #116

If offered a choice,
between a house or a vacation
choose the house.

You can go on vacation later.
Besides it's nice to come home from
vacation to your own home.

AB Survival Skill #117

Own a cocktail dress.

AB Survival Skill #118

Dream!

AB Survival Skill #119

Always have something in your life that motivates you.

AB Survival Skill #120

When a woman has a history she has nothing to lose.
But when she has the hope for a future she has to be careful.

(I cannot remember who told me this)

AB Survival Skill #121

Sometimes it's all about you!

AB Survival Skills
YOU
Self Evaluation

<u>What is your level of Ambitiousness?</u>
☐ 80% and more checked
☐ 50% - 79% checked
☐ Up to 49% checked
(See page 19 for definitions)

ಳು

1) Which three AB Survival Skills from chapter YOU do you want to master over the next six months?

1 – AB Survival Skill # _____

2 – AB Survival Skill # _____

3 – AB Survival Skill # _____

2) Which three AB Survival Skills from chapter YOU do you want to master over the next twelve months?

1 – AB Survival Skill # _____

2 – AB Survival Skill # _____

3 – AB Survival Skill # _____

3) Which is your favorite AB Survival Skill from chapter YOU? AB Survival Skill # _____

4) Which do you consider the most important AB Survival Skill from chapter YOU?
AB Survival Skill # _____

5) If you had to share just one AB Survival Skill from chapter YOU with your best friend, which one would you choose? AB Survival Skill # _____

   5a) Why would you choose this one?
   _____
   _____

6) It's your son or daughters first day of work, which two AB Survival Skills from chapter YOU do you send them off with?
AB Survival Skills # _____ & _____

7) Are you happy with your level of Ambitiousness? Yes or no.

   7a) If yes, beyond the level you achieved what do you like about your accomplishments in this section?_____
   _____

   7b) If no, what can you do to improve in this area? _____
   _____
   _____

Family

Definition of FAMILY

Family can have so many meanings.

It can be your blood relatives.
It can be your church family.
It can be your closest friends.

Whatever is your meaning, love is in the center of family.

AB Survival Skill #122

Priority # 1
is your family!

AB Survival Skill #123

There is a reason our children are "teenagers" before they are "adults."

Make sure they enjoy their teenage years.

AB Survival Skill #124

Start a college fund for your children as soon as possible.

AB Survival Skill #125

Naming your children is the first major
decision you will make for them.

Give it the thought and time
it is worth!

AB Survival Skill #126

Listen to your children.
They do know a thing or two!

Not everything has stayed
the same.

AB Survival Skill #127

Do not compare yourself with other family members.

They have what they have and that's nice. Develop your own goals, acquire your own assets, and do not compete with theirs.

AB Survival Skill #128

Teach your children to save!

AB Survival Skill #129

Your children turnout – for the most part – how you raised them.

So, if you do everything for your children, do not be surprised when they grow up to be dependent adults.

Or if you do nothing for your children, do not be surprised when they grow up and never call you.

Ambitious

Aspiring to achieve a particular goal.

AB Survival Skill #130

You do not have to win every argument with your spouse.
Sometimes losing is really a win!

AB Survival Skill #131

Remember, you will need to educate, clothe and feed each of the children you choose to have.

AB Survival Skill #132

In the presence of your children, treat your spouse the way you want your children to treat their current or future spouse.

Your ways will become their ways.

AB Survival Skill #133

Get up and go to work every day,
even when you don't feel like it.

Your children are watching and will see
and hopefully inherit this quality.

My friend Jackie

AB Survival Skill #134

Share your old favorites with your children!

AB Survival Skill #135

Call your parents!

AB Survival Skill #136

Having a child does not save
a marriage.

AB Survival Skill #137

If you are a single mother, embrace it.

AB Survival Skill #138

Your children are yours!

Do not rely on anyone else to raise them.
Help is great, but you are the parent.

AB Survival Skill #139

Try yoga.
It is an inexpensive way to good health.

AB Survival Skill #140

Teach your children manners.

They are not born with the information.

AB Survival Skill #141

Having children requires a sacrifice.

It is a sacrifice of your time.
It is a sacrifice of your money.
It is a sacrifice of you.

AB Survival Skill #142

If your children are away at college, make sure you visit them.
They may act or pretend like they don't miss you, but they will sleep better the night you leave.

AB Survival Skill #143

Teach healthy eating through gardening!
If you don't have a backyard, you can grow
tomatoes in a pot.

AB Survival Skill #144

If you are smarter than your husband, he knows it.
Don't dumb down!

AB Survival Skill #145

Your husband is just that – yours.

Don't share too much,
and trust no one

AB Survival Skill #146

You cannot pick your children's friends. You can only guide them to be selective in the friends they choose.

AB Survival Skill #147

If you explain the importance of a college
education to your children,
it will help with the transition from
high school.

AB Survival Skill #148

Confirm your children's knowledge. Never assume that they should "just" know.

AB Survival Skill #149

Attend as many as possible of your child's school plays, activities and sporting events.

AB Survival Skill #150

Bullies can be stopped at home!

It is not the school's responsibility to teach your child how to behave or how to handle situations...
that is your job!

PS: If they are not stopped as children, they grow up to be bullies in the workplace.

AB Survival Skill #151

You are not your child's
best friend.

You are their parent!

AB Survival Skill #152

It is okay to make more money than your husband!

AB Survival Skill #153

Always have your own money.

AB Survival Skill #154

What you did not like about your husband while dating, you will not like after you are married to him.

Do not wake up ten years later and complain.

AB Survival Skills
FAMILY
Self Evaluation

<u>What is your level of Ambitiousness?</u>
☐ 80% and more checked
☐ 50% - 79% checked
☐ Up to 49% checked
(See page 19 for definitions)

ଅ

1) Which three AB Survival Skills from chapter FAMILY do you want to master over the next six months?

1 – AB Survival Skill # _____

2 – AB Survival Skill # _____

3 – AB Survival Skill # _____

2) Which three AB Survival Skills from chapter FAMILY do you want to master over the next twelve months?

1 – AB Survival Skill # _____

2 – AB Survival Skill # _____

3 – AB Survival Skill # _____

3) Which is your favorite AB Survival Skill from chapter FAMILY? AB Survival Skill # _____

4) Which do you consider the most important AB Survival Skill from chapter FAMILY?
   AB Survival Skill # _____

5) If you had to share just one AB Survival Skill from chapter FAMILY with your daughter, niece or sister, which one would you choose?
   AB Survival Skill # _____

   5a) Why would you choose this one?
   _____
   _____

6) It's your son or daughters first day of college, which two AB Survival Skills from chapter FAMILY do you send them off with?
   AB Survival Skills # _____ & _____

7) Are you happy with your level of Ambitiousness? Yes or no.

   7a) If yes, beyond the level you achieved what do you like about your accomplishments in this section?_____
   _____

   7b) If no, what can you do to improve in this area _____
   _____
   _____

Love

Definition of LOVE

Love is an emotional connection towards another person.

AB Survival Skill #155

Always be in love!

AB Survival Skill #156

Do not act like you are married, before you are married.

My friend Jennifer

This can really scare him away!

AB Survival Skill #157

Everyone grows old.

Sex will stop one day, so marry someone you enjoy being with outside of the bed.

Remember intimacy can
last a lifetime!

AB Survival Skill #158

Men tend to love with their eyes first.

Women tend to love with
their hearts first.

Then we (men and women) turn 40 and a more practical eye takes focus.

Make sure you look twice before
you say "I do."

AB Survival Skill #159

If you pick men quicker than you select a pair of shoes… think again, and put some of them back on the shelf!

AB Survival Skill #160

Love can hurt!
But it can feel great too!

AB Survival Skill #161

When the man you are dating says he "has no money," be careful, because the next statement may be "can you spare a dime?"

AB Survival Skill #162

Don't forget that you were once single too!

AB Survival Skill #163

If you give the man you are dating the
whole "cookie jar"
what's left for him to want?

One cookie at a time, please!

AB Survival Skill #164

How he treats his mother is a very strong indication of
how he will treat you.

My friend Bob
A male point of view

This is more important than
if you like his mother.

AB Survival Skill #165

Take your time to plan the wedding of your dreams.

AB Survival Skill #166

Watch what you wear.
Leave something to his imagination.

My friend Ruby

AB Survival Skill #167

Love with all your heart,
and all your soul!

Just don't lose control!

AB Survival Skill #168

Remember if a man wants to be with you he will make the time.

Ambition

Demonstrating Effort.

AB Survival Skill #169

Know how your heart feels when it is warning you.

Know how your heart feels when it is satisfied and happy.

AB Survival Skill #170

Always remember the first time you fell in love!

AB Survival Skill #171

Know why "family" is important to you.

AB Survival Skill #172

Raise your son to be
emotionally balanced.

It's okay for men and boys to cry.

AB Survival Skill #173

If he never wants you to
meet his family –
you may not be the one.

AB Survival Skill #174

Become friends before you become husband and wife.

Note: He does not replace your girlfriends.

AB Survival Skill #175

Don't stress because he does not say those three little words.

AB Survival Skill #176

Unless you are certain about the health condition of the man you are with, always protect yourself.

Looks can be deceiving!
Clean on the outside, does not always mean clean on the inside!

AB Survival Skill #177

When dating know who you are to him!

My friend Garry
A male point of view

Do not assume you are more to him than he has stated.

AB Survival Skill #178

Know where your relationship
is at all times.

Are you casually dating or are you in an
exclusive relationship?

AB Survival Skill #179

If his family & friends warn you about him, take heed...
grab your coat and run!

My friend Ruby

AB Survival Skill #180

If a man wants you, he will accept you just as you are.

AB Survival Skill #181

If you do not want to have children, make this known as soon as
you think the relationship is
getting serious.

AB Survival Skill #182

Respect his POV!

My friend Ed
A male point of view

AB Survival Skill #183

The most important sex organ
is your brain.

My friend Joanna

AB Survival Skills
LOVE
Self Evaluation

<u>What is your level of Ambitiousness?</u>
☐ 80% and more checked
☐ 50% - 79% checked
☐ Up to 49% checked
(See page 19 for definitions)

ಸಿ

1) Which three AB Survival Skills from chapter LOVE do you want to master over the next six months?

1 – AB Survival Skill # _____

2 – AB Survival Skill # _____

3 – AB Survival Skill # _____

2) Which three AB Survival Skills from chapter LOVE do you want to master over the next twelve months?

1 – AB Survival Skill # _____

2 – AB Survival Skill # _____

3 – AB Survival Skill # _____

3) Which is your favorite AB Survival Skill from chapter LOVE? AB Survival Skill # _____

4) Which is your most important AB Survival Skill from chapter LOVE? AB Survival Skill # _____

5) If you had to share just one AB Survival Skill from chapter LOVE with your daughter who is getting married, which one would you choose?
AB Survival Skill # _____

   5a) Why would you choose this one?
   _____

6) Your best friend is always having boyfriend/husband troubles. Which two LOVE Survival Skills do you share with her?
AB Survival Skills # _____ & _____

7) Are you happy with your level of Ambitiousness? Yes or no.

   7a) If yes, beyond the level you achieved what do you like about your accomplishments in this section?_____
   _____

   7b) If no, what can you do to improve in this area? _____
   _____
   _____

Friends

Definition of a FRIEND

Someone you can trust, confine in and count on.

AB Survival Skill #184

You establish your reputation by the company you keep!

You establish your online reputation by what you allow people to expose. If you do not do it, it cannot be exposed.

Long gone are the days when you have to say "cheese" before your picture is taken!

AB Survival Skill #185

When a friendship ends,
understand why and move on.

Sometimes they are worth
trying to keep.

You cannot determine this unless you
understand why it ended.

AB Survival Skill #186

If you allow their negative remarks and comments to bother you,
"they" are in control.

AB Survival Skill #187

Tell your friends the truth.

You can do this without being rude, harsh or nasty.

AB Survival Skill #188

Be willing to listen to others' opinions and points of view.

Even if you don't agree it is important to understand different perspectives.

My friend and protégé Lillian

AB Survival Skill #189

A new car only impresses your friends
the first time they see it,
or when they need a ride.

AB Survival Skill #190

Define your enemies.
All of them.

Once on this list…
always on this list.

AB Survival Skill #191

Define how your friends can
help you grow and know how you can
help them grow too.

AB Survival Skill #192

Understand why you call someone a friend.

AB Survival Skill #193

Understand why someone calls you their friend.

AB Survival Skill #194

Do not compare your friends
to each other.

They are each beautiful and wonderful!

AB Survival Skill #195

Host a dinner party for no reason.

AB Survival Skill #196

When a friend is down, do not go down with them.

They need you to stand tall so they can climb back out.

AB Survival Skill #197

People don't change.

AB Survival Skill #198

Know when to compromise and when to stand firm.

My friend and protégé Sarah

AB Survival Skill #199

You do not need to win every battle.

AB Survival Skill #200

Admire the older woman who knows that she is older and loves it!

AB Survival Skill #201

Accept apologies quickly and with grace, and then move on.

AB Survival Skill #202

Have at least one friend who makes you better.

Knowing what knowledge, skills and connections your friends have should be added to your list of accessible assets.

AB Survival Skill #203

Remember the important dates in your friends lives.

AB Survival Skill #204

Define what you bring to each friendship.

AB Survival Skill #205

Define how your enemies can help you.

AB Survival Skill #206

Understand why someone is your enemy.

Ambition

The desire to achieve great things!

AB Survival Skill #207

Admire, but do not be jealous of women who are younger than you.

AB Survival Skill #208

Love your friends' children!

AB Survival Skill #209

Never take sides between two friends.

AB Survival Skill #210

Do not compare yourself
to your friends.

AB Survival Skill #211

Do not compete with your friends.

AB Survival Skill #212

If you have friends that are much younger then you, remember their stuff will go south too!

AB Survival Skill #213

Separate friends from acquaintances.

AB Survival Skill #214

Know which friends can spread information fast.

Know how they will spread that information.

Having a friend that cannot keep a secret is not necessarily a bad thing as long a you understand this about them.

AB Survival Skills
FRIENDS
Self Evaluation

<u>What is your level of Ambitiousness?</u>

☐ 80% and more checked

☐ 50% - 79% checked

☐ Up to 49% checked

(See page 19 for definitions)

1) Which three AB Survival Skills from chapter FRIENDS do you want to master over the next six months?

1 – AB Survival Skill # ________________

2 – AB Survival Skill # ________________

3 – AB Survival Skill # ________________

2) Which three AB Survival Skills from chapter FRIENDS do you want to master over the next twelve months?

1 – AB Survival Skill # ________________

2 – AB Survival Skill # ________________

3 – AB Survival Skill # ________________

3) Which is your favorite AB Survival Skill from chapter FRIENDS? AB Survival Skill # __________

4) Which is your most important AB Survival Skill from chapter FRIENDS?
AB Survival Skill # _____

5) If you had to share just one AB Survival Skill from chapter FRIENDS with your best friend, which one would you choose? AB Survival Skill # _____

   5a) Why would you choose this one?
   _____
   _____

6) It's your son or daughter's sixteenth birthday, which two AB Survival Skills from chapter FRIENDS do you share with them on this day?
AB Survival Skills # _____ & _____

7) Are you happy with your level of Ambitiousness? Yes or no.

   7a) If yes, beyond the level you achieved what do you like about your accomplishments in this section? _____
   _____

   7b) If no, what can you do to improve in this area? _____
   _____
   _____

Work

Definition of WORK

For the purposes of this book, "work" is your place of employment.

AB Survival Skill #215

Be on time.

Being respectably late only works when you are going to a party.

On the job, it will get you fired!

AB Survival Skill #216

Research the company before you go on an interview.

Taking the time to do this will assist you in developing your questions for the interview.

AB Survival Skill #217

Take lots of notes at meetings.
If you are bored,
pretend to take lots of notes.

It is always important to look engaged.

AB Survival Skill #218

Develop loyalties to
your co-workers.

AB Survival Skill #219

Job hopping really does not get you anywhere.

AB Survival Skill #220

If you wake up one day and realize that you have a department of people under you that cannot make a decision, you should also realize that you have exactly what you have developed.

AB Survival Skill #221

When you go on a job interview, remember that you are interviewing the company too.

AB Survival Skill #222

When going on an interview, always dress for success.

Save your business casual clothes for after you get the job.

AB Survival Skill #223

Define your friends at work.

AB Survival Skill #224

Good things come to those who WORK!

AB Survival Skill #225

Make sure you are prepared for that job interview.

Take the time to research the company your have an interview with. By taking the time to do this, you may realize in advance that you do not wish to work for that company.

AB Survival Skill #226

Do not think your boss should know more than you.

AB Survival Skill #227

Always have expectations, goals and objectives.

They help form the path to your future.

AB Survival Skill #228

If you ever wonder how your boss got
their position –
look at the person who
gave it to them!

AB Survival Skill #229

Meetings should begin and
end on time.

AB Survival Skill #230

If you call a meeting,
have an agenda.

AB Survival Skill #231

Your resume should
always be ready.

Proofread it,
and then proofread it again.
A typo can cost you a job.

AB Survival Skill #232

When you get promoted from Manager to Director or Vice President, remember you are no longer
a Manager.

How you direct people
should change.

AB Survival Skill #233

Always arrive early to work, and never leave on time.

AB Survival Skill #234

Remember: Your performance review for
the most part –
is the opinion of the person
who prepared it.

If you value their opinion, take note of their comments, and work towards improvement.

On the other hand, if you do not value their opinion, make the necessary corrections to save your job, but do not lose any sleep!

AB Survival Skill #235

Who's the boss?
Know who really makes
the decisions.

PS: It's not always the person in charge,
or the person with the
highest position.

AB Survival Skill #236

Keep a work journal.
You cannot remember everything.

AB Survival Skill #237

If you are a manager, ask yourself the following question:

What survival skills do you teach the people who work for you?

AB Survival Skill #238

Say "good morning" to everyone.

AB Survival Skill #239

Define how you can help each of your friends at work.

Ambitious

Desire to work.

AB Survival Skill #240

Make sure you know the personalities of your co-workers.

AB Survival Skill #241

Dress for success.

AB Survival Skill #242

When asked for your opinion, give it politely and professionally,
and never apologize for it.

AB Survival Skill #243

Micromanaging is never pretty!

Being micromanaged can limit your success!

Being a micromanager can burn you out!

AB Survival Skill #244

Take lunch. You need to refuel!

No one is impressed that you work through lunch!

AB Survival Skill #245

Remember when you work for someone else,
it is not your money.

They have the right to choose how to spend it.

AB Survival Skill #246

If your boss is an idiot,
work really hard.
(Should not take too much effort)

Why?

Because somebody likes them and they
may go far.

AB Survival Skill #247

The inability to make a decision will hold you back.

It will also make you appear insecure.

AB Survival Skill #248

Bullies grow up and get jobs.

They are sometimes your co-worker, direct report or boss.

Make it known that you are not prey.

AB Survival Skill #249

Always be prepared to take
over your boss's job.

AB Survival Skill #250

Know your strengths and
keep them strong.

AB Survival Skill #251

Know your weaknesses and work on them.

AB Survival Skill #252

Your "at work" husband is
not a bad thing!

He is a really good friend!

Note: This is <u>not</u> an affair.

AB Survival Skill #253

Do not expect to like your boss.

If you do, it's a bonus!

AB Survival Skill #254

Make sure someone else can do your job, so you can move ahead.

AB Survival Skill #255

As a manager, never allow whether or not the people you manage like you or not to consume you.

Of course, it helps if they like you.

Make sure you are fair, honest, true to yourself and of course available.

AB Survival Skills
WORK
Self Evaluation

What is your level of Ambitiousness?
☐ 80% and more checked
☐ 50% - 79% checked
☐ Up to 49% checked
(See page 19 for definitions)

☙

1) Which three AB Survival Skills from chapter WORK do you want to master over the next six months?

1 – AB Survival Skill # _____

2 – AB Survival Skill # _____

3 – AB Survival Skill # _____

2) Which three AB Survival Skills from chapter WORK do you want to master over the next twelve months?

1 – AB Survival Skill # _____

2 – AB Survival Skill # _____

3 – AB Survival Skill # _____

3) Which is your favorite AB Survival Skill from chapter WORK? AB Survival Skill # _____

4) Which is your most important AB Survival Skill from chapter WORK? AB Survival Skill # _____

5) If you had to share just one AB Survival Skill from chapter WORK with a co-worker, which one would you choose? AB Survival Skill # _____

   5a) Why would you choose this one?
   _____

6) Which two AB Survival Skills from chapter WORK do you Share with your protégé?
   AB Survival Skills # _____ & _____

7) Are you happy with your level of Ambitiousness? Yes or no.

   7a) If yes, beyond the level you achieved what do you like about your accomplishments in this section?_____
   _____

   7b) If no, what can you do to improve in this area?_____
   _____
   _____

Faith

Definition of FAITH

Faith is how you believe.

AB Survival Skill #256

Have faith!

AB Survival Skill #257

Do not spend on faith!

AB Survival Skill #258

Give.

AB Survival Skill #259

Say "God bless you"

Bless you is just not enough!

AB Survival Skill #260

No matter your history, there is a greater future!

God loves you too much!

AB Survival Skill #261

Say grace or
give thanks before each meal!

AB Survival Skill #262

Fellowship is important!

AB Survival Skill #263

Give thanks to God... every day!

AB Survival Skill #264

He may not come when
you want him, but He is
always right on time.

(Sure you've heard this before!)

AB Survival Skill #265

If you do not like the church or place of worship you are going to,
do not stop going, find a new one.

AB Survival Skill #266

Faith requires action.

AB Survival Skill #267

Don't give up!

AB Survival Skill #268

Remember, each day is a blessing!

Ambitious

To try!

AB Survival Skill #269

Share your blessings.

AB Survival Skill #270

Be a blessing to someone.

AB Survival Skill #271

Own a Bible.

AB Survival Skill #272

Believe!

AB Survival Skill #273

Face your giants!

AB Survival Skill #274

When you give it to God,
leave it there.

AB Survival Skill #275

Make your prayers clear!

Do not be afraid to ask for what you want.

AB Survival Skill #276

Pray with faith and confidence.

NOTE: It doesn't hurt to be specific.

AB Survival Skill #277

The time is NOW to believe
what God says.

AB Survival Skill #278

Step out on faith
and let the Lord use you!

AB Survival Skill #279

What's your favorite uplifting movie?
Mine is "Facing the Giants".

A movie about strength and faith!

A movie about strength and faith!

AB Survival Skill #280

It's not our place to question why!

AB Survival Skill #281

Thank God for what you have.

My friend Trina

AB Survival Skill #282

Forgive so you can move on.

Holding on to "stuff" will weight you down and age you!

AB Survival Skill #283

Recognize when grace and mercy are gifted upon you.

AB Survival Skill #284

Be faithful to your faith!

AB Survival Skill #285

Go to church!

AB Survival Skill #286

Have a Holy Ghost party!
People will come!

AB Survival Skill #287

Recognize when you are climbing up a mountain and when you are going down the mountain.

Sometimes we get caught up in the climb and fail to feel the change in the slope.

AB Survival Skills
FAITH
Self Evaluation

What is your level of Ambitiousness?
- ☐ 80% and more checked
- ☐ 50% - 79% checked
- ☐ Up to 49% checked

(See page 19 for definitions)

ഇ

1) Which three AB Survival Skills from chapter FAITH do you want to master over the next six months?

1 – AB Survival Skill # _____

2 – AB Survival Skill # _____

3 – AB Survival Skill # _____

2) Which three AB Survival Skills from chapter FAITH do you want to master over the next twelve months?

1 – AB Survival Skill # _____

2 – AB Survival Skill # _____

3 – AB Survival Skill # _____

3) Which is your favorite AB Survival Skill from chapter FAITH? AB Survival Skill # _____

4) Which is your most important AB Survival Skill from chapter FAITH? AB Skill # _____

5) If you had to share just one AB Survival Skill from chapter FAITH with a church friend, which one would you choose? AB Survival Skill # _____

   5a) Why would you choose this one?
   _____

6) If you were asked to give a lecture to the women's group at your church, which two AB Survival Skills from chapter FAITH will you select?
AB Survival Skill # _____ & _____

7) Are you happy with your level of Ambitiousness? Yes or no.

   7a) If yes, beyond the level you achieved what do you like about your accomplishments in this section?_____
   _____

   7b) If no, what can you do to improve in this area? _____
   _____
   _____

Once upon a time…

during a meeting,
while making a point,
one of my co-workers said to the person
sitting next to them
"Wow, she's a real "b----"!

I politely turned to that
co-worker and said

"No, I am just AMBITIOUS!"

Join The AB Club
Membership is $15.00

Includes

- **Blog Spot Highlight by Michelle**
  Let Michelle highlight your company, business and you in her Blog.

- **Bragging rights that you are a member of *The AB Club!***

- **Purchase any of Michelle's books at the AB Club member discount.**
  This special offer is available through mail order only from Blaque Design, Inc.

Send check or money order for membership and books to:
Blaque Design, LLC
P.O. Box 1527
Jackson NJ 08527

Remember to include the following with your order:
- Your shipping address
- Information about your company, business and you
  (You can email this to michelle@michellewinfrey.com)
- Your email address
- If purchasing books include quantity by title

Purchase books by Michelle Whitaker Winfrey

Title	Regular Price	Discount Price	AB Club Price
The AB Club For the Am-Bitious Woman in You!	$14.99	$12.00	$10.00
A Moms Guide to Surviving High School Athletics	$21.99	$18.00	$15.00
Yours, Mine and Gods Giving and Receiving All for the Love of God and the Church	$16.99	$14.00	$10.00
It's My Birthday... Finally! A Leap Year Story	$11.95	$10.00	$8.00
It's My Birthday... Finally! Activity & Workbook	$10.95	$9.00	$7.00
It's Not Leap Year this Year! A Leap Year Story	$11.95	$10.00	$8.00

Shipping Information for books
$4.00 first book
.50 cents each additional book.

If you are not joining *The AB Club*, books may be purchased at the discount price.

For The AB Club Apparel

www.cafepress.com/ABClub

Shirts, Bags, Mugs
and more!

Wear your Ambitiousness!
Show off your Ambitiousness!

www.ingramcontent.com/pod-product-compliance
Lightning Source LLC
LaVergne TN
LVHW041610070426
835507LV00008B/181